The
Great Fire
in St. John's, Newfoundland
July 8, 1892

by
Rev. Moses Harvey
and
A Bostonian Visitor

with an introduction by
Fred Adams

The Great Fire in St. John's, Newfoundland July 8, 1892

by
Rev. Moses Harvey
and
A Bostonian Visitor

with an introduction by
Fred Adams

Creative Publishers
St. John's, Newfoundland
1992

Appreciation is expressed to *The Canada Council* for publication assistance.

The publisher acknowledges the financial contribution of the *Department of Tourism and Culture, Government of Newfoundland and Labrador*, which has helped make this publication possible.

∝Printed on acid-free "Sno-Glo" offset paper

Published by
CREATIVE PUBLISHERS
A Division of Robinson-Blackmore Printing & Publishing Ltd.
P.O. Box 8660, St. John's, Newfoundland A1B 3T7

Printed in Canada by
ROBINSON-BLACKMORE PRINTING & PUBLISHING LTD.
P.O. Box 8660, St. John's, Newfoundland A1B 3T7

ISBN 1-895387-16-7

1992 is the one-hundredth anniversary of what St. John's residents have come to call "The Great Fire." The story has been told and retold, but never more eloquently than in this early account, first published in 1892.

Many people in St. John's today will remember having been told first-hand accounts of the conflagration by their parents and/or grandparents. Fred Adams falls into this category, and we are pleased that he has brought this manuscript to our attention. He has also provided the photographs to support the text, and the recollections that bring the photographs to life.

We hope you will appreciate the story as it unfolds here through words written one hundred years ago, and also that you will come to value the generous spirit and commitment of ordinary people, who helped the city to rise, phoenix-like, from its ashes.

The Publisher

Contents

Acknowledgements

In this book many people have been very helpful and considerate, and in this connection I would like to thank the following:

Mr. Willis Brady, who provided an original 1892 report by the special appeal committee of Boston and surrounding cities and towns;

Captain Bill Rossiter of the St. John's Fire Department, a friend of many years;

Mr. Paul Sears, archivist, curator, historian and veteran fire fighter, of seventeen years in the department;

And finally, Mr. Don Morgan of Creative Publishers and Mr. Bill Callahan of *The Evening Telegram*.

Introduction

Although the Great Fire of July 8, 1892 occurred twenty-six years before I was born, it has had a pronounced impact on my life—especially since my becoming a serious student of St. John's history. It has been discussed by our family many times. Fortunately our house was far removed from the source of the fire, but many survivors—mainly relatives—were housed with my grandparents until alternative accommodation could be found. One of my grandfather's nephews actually built a house in our back meadow.

Much has been written about the Great Fire, and through reading about it and hearing the stories, it seems almost as though I lived through it myself. My father told me that as children, he and his older sisters stood on a small cliff at the top of Rocky Lane—now Prince of Wales Street—and watched the city burning. Some members of our family lived on Carter's Hill and were burned out along with many other unfortunate families.

The fall season was fast approaching and great haste was required to make sure that there was enough shelter for everyone before the cold weather set in. A total of 1572 houses were razed to the ground, leaving more than 11,000 people without shelter. I believe this book conveys some of the feeling of despair and hopelessness that must have prevailed when the homeless realized the gravity of their situation. Imagine how a father or mother with small children must have felt when their home and all or most of its contents went up in flames, followed by the realization that the breadwinner's job had also disappeared because his place of employment was in all likelihood gone as well. Obviously an appalling situation existed, and immediate measures were required to cope with such devastation. Hundreds of tents were erected in the various meadows and fields throughout the town to provide temporary shelter while the city caught its breath so to speak, and a great building program was soon in the making.

As a direct result of the fire most industry was brought to an abrupt stand-still. The fishing industry and most of the related spin-off jobs—sail and net lofts, iron work, forges, cooperages—the fire had a ripple effect on all these industries. Ships chandlers and marine supply merchants were wiped out. Sheds and warehouses, wharves and finger piers, were burnt to the water's edge. The effect was even felt in the outlying, undamaged areas of the city, for although the businesses on the outskirts survived, their immediate market had been effectively removed.

As far as the sealing industry was concerned however, there was one redeeming feature; all the sealing properties were located on the southside of the harbour which had escaped the flames. On the other hand, many St. John's men were forced to refuse berths to the ice the following spring, because of commitments at home due to the fire.

Following the fire most men in St. John's—tradesmen and unskilled alike—were soon kept busy at building houses, stores, sheds, wharves and buildings of every description. A large number of men who were employed in places such as Boston, New York, Philadelphia and as far away as the Boulder Dam project in Colorado returned to St. John's to help in the rebuilding. Many skilled men employed as riggers and steeplejacks, bridge builders and other skilled workers—all making good wages—arrived home voluntarily to help in the work, at much lower wages than they had been making, in order to assist fire victims and relatives who had been burned out.

A monumental effort was put forth by the citizens of St. John's to help each other, and with the aid in goods and money generously provided by Halifax, Boston and outlying towns and cities, the city succeeded in having most victims under a roof of some sort in time for winter. St. john's possessed very little equipment to cope with a disaster of such magnitude, and practically every piece of rubble had to be removed by hand and carried away in wheel barrows, hand barrows and by horse and cart. Much of the brick and a good deal of lumber was salvaged, to be recycled into the homes and buildings being erected. In a disaster of such proportions everyone is brought to the same level, and cooperation becomes a necessity. The citizens of St. John's proved up to the task, and as a result we have the beautiful city we enjoy today, one hundred years later.

It is my opinion that to this day a debt of gratitude is owed by the people of St. John's to the people of Boston and the surrounding area, New York, Halifax and other cities. In our hour of need they—many of them expatriate Newfoundlanders—provided an outpouring of money, food and other necessities as they rallied to the cause.

To quote from the executive committee that was formed in the city of Boston "Here was a city, prosperous, intelligent and powerful, almost obliterated in a few hours." The committee organized the city and its environs to render what aid and assistance it could; they forwarded almost $16,000 in money and goods, a significant sum one hundred years ago.

A native of St. John's residing in Boston, a young poet named Henry O'Meara, composed a touching poem which appears further on in this book, adding to the value of Reverend Harvey's work. Also, the committee under chairman Taylor in Boston, displays in the most eloquent terms the compassion of the Newfoundland expatriate for those at home.

For the most part this book is a reprint of the report published by the committee under the chairmanship of the Hon. William Taylor. Much of the work and the history contained herein is due to the effort of Reverend Moses Harvey, who was an eye-witness to the fire. I am merely endeavouring to bring the narrative together with this introduction, and a collection of photographs to enhance the text.

FRED ADAMS

JULY 1992

SALUTATORY

The terrible conflagration at St. John's, Newfoundland, whereby from $15,000,000 to $20,000,000 of property was wiped out of existence by the fire fiend in a few hours and 10,000 people left homeless has shocked and pained the civilized world. Here was a city prosperous, intelligent, and powerful, almost obliterated in a few hours.

Boston forwarded, in money and goods, nearly $16,000; all these gifts coming in with sympathy and heartiness that made them doubly acceptable. Of this effort of relief, and of the calamity which called it forth, the following pages are published as a memorial record.

To all who contributed to this worthy cause the Executive Committee, on behalf of the fire sufferers, return their most grateful thanks. St. John's has from the inception of her history enjoyed a world-wide reputation for the generosity of its people—an appeal made to them for the relief of others had never once been unheeded. So, in turn, while the fire was smouldering in the ruins of the fairest portion of their city, relief came pouring in from the outside world through every available channel.

The history of the fire contained in this volume is the work of the Rev. Moses Harvey, well known to all lovers of the Island, author of a history of Newfoundland and a writer of wide repute on natural history and other subjects. He had the mournful privilege of seeing the beginning, the terrifying growth, and the tardy arrest of the conflagration. His account of it gives a literary and historic value to this *Souvenir;* while the contribution of Mr. Henry O'Meara, our young Boston poet, himself a native of the city of St. John's, still adds to its value.

In addition to this our generous friends will find herein an account of our stewardship, with credit given to every contributor whose name could be ascertained.

THE EXECUTIVE COMMITTEE

St. John's is still smouldering in this photograph, taken July 9, 1892, the day following the fire.

ORGANIZATION

On saturday morning, July 8, the newspapers of Boston contained the startling intelligence that the city of St. John's, Newfoundland, was swept by fire the previous night. On the following Sunday evening a number of Newfoundlanders met at America Hall, and after talking over the sad news and pledging their assistance, adjourned to meet on the following Thursday evening. Meanwhile every person present promised to interest himself in reaching Newfoundlanders living in outlying towns and cities, informing them of the meeting to be held, and, if possible, to secure their presence on that evening. As a result the largest body of Newfoundlanders ever brought together at one meeting in the city of Boston met at America Hall, on Thursday evening, July 14. The permanent organization was as follows:

Chairman.—Hon. William Taylor.

Secretary.—William Whittle.

Treasurer.—Edward T. Russell.

Assistant Treasurer.—John G. Pike.

Financial Secretary.—Robert J. Druhan.

Executive Committee.

Hon. William Taylor,
William Whittle,
Edward T. Russell,
John G. Pike,
Robert J. Druhan,
John P. McCormick,
Rev. A.B. Hudson,
M.M. Breen,
Nicholas Sullivan,
Thomas Kevin,
Thomas Higgins,
John W. O'Ryan.

Committees were appointed in the following cities and towns from among the Newfoundlanders residing therein:

Brighton.—Matthew Murphy, Chairman; William Cunningham, M. Rielly, M.M. Breen, J. Kennedy, John Foley, Michael Murphy.

Brockton.—Alexander Morton, Chairman; Thomas Brien, Thomas J. Regan.

Cambridgeport.—Dr. Jos. D. Couch.

Charlestown.—Michael Rogers, Chairman; F. Fleming, Garrett Dooley, James Dooley, James Britt, Michael Manning.

Chelsea.—Archibald Prior, Chairman; John Power, Herbert Dowden, Thomas Parsons, Richard Parsons, Stephen Breaker.

East Boston.—M.J. Crotty, Chairman; Daniel Kiley, Thomas Ryan, Nicholas J. Ryan, Edward Gardiner, Richard Power, Michael Fitzgerald.

East Cambridge.—John P. McCormick, Chairman; Peter Shortell, John Gleason.

Everett.—James Bolger, Chairman; E.M. Archibald, Thomas Kenney, Charles Wilson, James McAuliffe, James W. Childs.

Lynn.—Robert Evans, Chairman; Harry Mews, P.J. Murphy, Joseph Pike.

Malden.—William Barrett.

Milville.—Patrick Heneberry, Chairman; Charles Duffey, William Mountain, William Parnell, Robert Powell, Richard Glynn, Michael Ryan.

Newton.—Richard J. Morrissey, Chairman; M. Moore, P.J. Powers.

North End.—Edward Walsh, Chairman; Thomas Kevin, P.J. Cody, Patrick Bowe, Peter Hogan, Thomas Fitzgerald, T. Lee.

Old Cambridge.—Gilbert Pynn, Chairman; W. Eastman, E.M. Phelan.

Quincy.—David Fitzgerald, Chairman.

Roxbury.—John T. McCarthy, Chairman; John J. Hally, P.J. Brazil, John T. Kennedy, Andrew Hughes, Thomas Lanahan, James Smart.

Somerville.—Edward Pynn, Chairman; Joseph G. Gallishaw, Robert J. Druhan, John Cotter.

South Boston.—Dennis J. Cantwell, Chairman; P.J. Feehan, Louis J. Duchemin, James L. Fitzgerald, Thomas Burns, Michael J. Renison, John F. Dempsey.

South End.—William Whittle, Chairman; P.J. Mansfield, M.W. Dooley, Thomas Mackay, Thomas Morrissey, D.J. Reddin.

The committees went to work with a determination to realize a handsome sum for the suffers, and they succeeded admirably, having collected in money and clothing (new clothing alone entering into this estimate) the sum of $15,896.80.* On Saturday afternoon, Aug. 6, the schooner *Carita* sailed for St. John's, chartered by the Executive Committee, and having on board a miscellaneous cargo of provisions and merchandise valued at $8,000. On October 18 the schooner *Alta* was despatched. By her the Committee sent 625 barrels of flour and other breadstuffs. It should be said here that the $3,460 collected by Messrs. Stratton, Little, & Co. and Edward T. Russell was sent by them to St. John's in cash.

* In terms of 1992 dollars, this would be about $300,000.

This interesting photo shows Water Street not long after the fire. You will notice that the wharves were burnt to the water's edge.

An Appeal*

The friends of Newfoundland appeal to the people of Boston in behalf of the chief city of that country, suffering now what may be a mortal calamity. Boston's aid has always been freely given to her suffering neighbors.

St. John's is a city of something over thirty thousand inhabitants, largely engaged in the fisheries. Shops of merchants and artisans are in ashes, so that work on shore is gone. At this season the fishermen are off along the coast, down to Labrador, or out on the banks, working hard that they may be able to lay by something for the hard winter. They have left at home their wives and children and the helpless old. They will get news of the fire from passing vessels, and whether they hasten home or not, what hope have they?

These sad and scanty details help out the meaning of Sunday morning's news that fifteen thousand people are homeless, and twenty million dollars' worth of property destroyed.

What can Boston do? Send food. St. John's is nearer than Russia. St. John's is your neighbor. Her sons are your fellow-citizens. Her working people are out of work, homeless, and starving. She needs and asks your help, and Boston is old at the business of charity. Aid in any shape will be acceptable. We are prepared to take care of any contributions given in money, clothing, or the necessities of life. All assistance will be thankfully received at the headquarters of the Relief Committee, 143 Harrison Avenue, where the Secretary will be in daily attendance from 8 A.M. to 8 P.M.

WILLIAM TAYLOR, *Chairman.*

WILLIAM WHITTLE, *Secretary.*

---

* This is the Appeal that was sent out from headquarters by the Executive Committee to the people of Boston and vicinity.

This is what St. John's looked like before the fire. The majority of these buildings, and all of those in the immediate foreground, were destroyed.

The Great Fire

Full details of the awful conflagration of July 8th, by which two-thirds of the city of St. John's was destroyed, have already appeared in the public press. I am requested, however, to furnish a brief description of the fire, which may be attached to the list of contributors in Boston to the Relief Fund, and I willingly comply with this request.

On the afternoon of that dark day in the annals of Newfoundland I attended a meeting in the basement of St. Andrew's Church, for the distribution of prizes to the pupils of the General Protestant Academy. Little did I imagine that this would be the last meeting in that fine, substantial building, and that when I next saw it, only shattered walls and smoke-begrimed ruins would greet the eye.

The meeting closed at a quarter past four, and in company with a friend I went for a walk in the direction of the Parade Ground. About five o'clock I noticed the glare of fire some distance beyond, near Freshwater Road, and hastening to the spot I found three houses on fire. I remarked to my friend that this was a bad day for a fire. A high wind from the north-west was blowing, hurling the sparks far and wide on the roofs of the clusters of wooden houses. For a month previous hardly any rain had fallen, and the shingled roofs were like tinder. The firemen were soon on the spot, but the supply of water was feeble, and their efforts to arrest the progress of the flames produced little effect. By a strange fatality the water had been turned off in the morning in order to make some new connections of mains, and though it had been turned on again its force on this high ground was slight. A tank which was usually full had been emptied the previous evening by the firemen, when practising with their hose, and by some stupid carelessness had not been filled.

Soon half a dozen more houses were on fire, then twenty. The volume of flames increased, and the roaring

The Terra Nova
In this interesting photograph in front of the Colonial Building, we see the first steam fire engine in Newfoundland. This photo was taken in 1885, seven years before the Great Fire.
Drawn by a splendid pair of horses, this unit was an impressive sight as the horses galloped to the scene of a fire. The driver seen here with whip in hand was looked on with awe and envy by the boys of the day. What a great pity that some of this beautiful and unique equipment was not preserved for posterity.
The horses usually shone from being brushed, and with the hooves blackened and harness in immaculate condition, they were the pride of St. John's.

wind hurled the burning brands in all directions, which, alighting on roofs at a distance, created fresh centres of fire. Then it became evident that an alarming conflagration had broken out, but no one yet dreamed of the terrible results that were to follow. The force of the wind was increased by the heat, and the fire was now steadily eating its way down Long's Hill into the very heart of the city. The firemen were overpowered, their hose burned, and the flames got beyond control. On the high ground to the right of Long's Hill stood a mass of wooden buildings, consisting of the Methodist College and schools, with dwelling-houses, the Masonic Temple, and the Presbyterian manse. In a few minutes the roof of the college began to smoke, and in half an hour the whole group of buildings was an enormous mass of flames. The fiery torrent, thus swollen, now rushed on, growing by what it fed on. The Methodist Gower Street Church, the Orange Hall, the Synod Hall and schools of the Church of England, the residence of Bishop Jones, went down before the avalanche of fire; and now the beautiful Cathedral of the Church of England—the pride of the city—was surrounded by a ring of flames. No one imagined that such a solid stone structure could be burned; and for an hour before the terrified people around had been carrying their valuables to it as a place of safety. Bishop Jones had placed in it all his household treasures. The fiery tornado swept on. The intense heat melted the lead around the panes of glass, and the destroyer having found an entrance, the stately Cathedral, with all its contents, was soon a glowing mass of fire. The beautifully moulded arches and massive pillars crumbled, and with a crash the lofty roof fell in. The flames leaped up, as if exulting, a hundred feet into the air, and resumed their destructive march. Now came the turn of St. Andrew's Presbyterian Church, which was only two or three hundred yards below the Cathedral. It was a massive brick building and supposed to be invulnerable to fire from outside; but the fierce heat soon melted the glass of the windows, and in an incredible short space of time nothing remained of St. Andrew's but the tower and blackened walls, shattered as with shot and shell.

Opposite St. Andrew's Church stood the Athenaeum. Desperate efforts were made to save it, but all in vain. It was a handsome structure, containing a fine concert and lecture hall, the Savings Bank, the Surveyor General's office, a public library, containing seven thousand volumes. The cost of the building was $60,000. It was the institution on which the city prided itself most, and indeed it would have been a credit to any community.

The ruins of the Congregational church. Note the harbour beacon light, which escaped damage.

The fiery giant rushed on. The Court-House, the Commercial Bank, with the surrounding buildings, speedily shared the common fate. The Union Bank made a stout resistance, and being favorably situated, and well protected by iron shutters, managed to escape. The conflagration now set to work on Duckworth Street, and soon it had all the streets above it in its grasp. Garrison Hill had gone some time before, and all efforts proved futile to save St. Patrick's fine hall, with the schools of the Christian Brothers on its ground floor. The Congregational Church, at no great distance, speedily succumbed; and all the area of houses in front of the Catholic Cathedral and onward towards the east end of the city furnished food for the flames.

The destroying force which had started so advantageously from the heights about the head of Long's Hill, overlooking the city, had here divided itself and sent a strong detachment down towards Water Street, a little east of Carter's Lane. Ere long this column burst into Water Street—the business part of the city—at Beck's Cove, cutting it in two, and leaving one-third untouched to the westward. Now the work of destruction commenced in earnest. Bowring's huge premises, shops, stores, warehouse, wharves, were soon enveloped in sheets of flame. The beautiful shops, full of valuable goods; the stores behind, containing thousands of barrels of flour and provision of all kinds; the fish stores; the wharves, which it had cost immense sums to erect,—disappeared one by one into the maw of the destroyer. Goodfellow's, Ayre & Sons', Baird's, Baine Johnston's, Thorburn & Tessier's, immense premises; Marshall & Roger's, Job Brothers' great block,—all fell a prey to the flames, and the whole of Water Street, on both sides, was "swept with the besom of destruction."

I had been watching the progress of the fire down Long's Hill and afterwards as it spread to Scotland Row and attacked the Cathedral and St. Patrick's Hall, and I had been helping some friends to remove their goods.

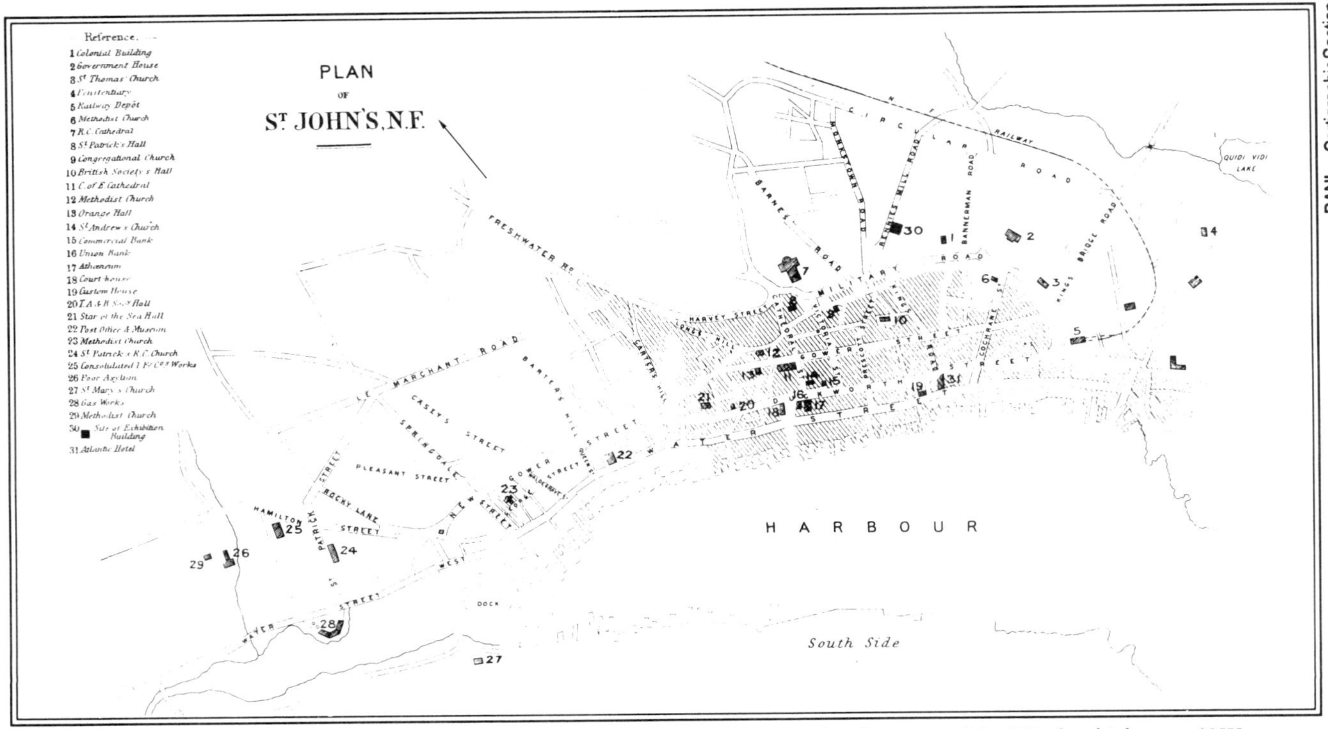

The Numbers show the Public Buildings that were burned.—The Arrow shows the direction of the Wind, which was N.W. The shaded portion shows the burned area.

PANL—Cartigraphic Section

When I saw that it had burst into Water Street and was sending out great flakes of fire and tornadoes of fiery particles, like an advanced host of skirmishers, while the solid mass of fire steadily advanced, I then knew that the city was doomed. I began to think of my own home in Devon Row, and for the first time realized that in all probability it would be included in the general destruction. Through a suffocating atmosphere, laden with burning sparks and blinding smoke, I wended my way homeward, and found that all the inhabitants of Devon Row were packing their goods and preparing to remove them to places of safety, as it was believed to be impossible to save the Row. I followed the general example, and we continued the work for two hours and a half, and were successful in carrying to a place of safety all that was portable—thanks to the aid of numerous kind friends. Meantime the fiery torrent was bearing straight down upon us. Devon Row consists of six brick houses, four stories in height, with a tarred asphalt roof—a projecting wooden cornice under the roof, and a wooden balcony behind, so that it presented many vulnerable points. The inmates were all doing their best to fight the fire, and a strong force was assembled at No. 5, the house next the fire. The roof was kept wet—wet blankets, placed at the end of the balcony, and brooms in active service to sweep off the sparks as they fell in myriads. Still, we had little hope of escaping, as far stronger buildings and better protected had perished. The torrent approached; the house next the Row blazed up, and the blood-red tongues of fire shot out, licking the gable-end and mounting towards the roof. We stood looking on, expecting every moment to see the roof or the windows on fire. We held our breath, waiting for the final catastrophe; but the fiery bombardment did not take effect; the sparks flew off without getting a lodgment; the flames from the burning house next it began to collapse after the roof fell in, and with a sigh of relief we realized that Devon Row was saved.

This is probably the most familiar photograph of the Great Fire. It was taken some time after the fire (note the temporary structures attached to the existing chimneys). It shows in devastating detail the complete and utter destruction of the city. Almost nothing was left standing.

Had it gone, all the houses below it, with the railway station, would have been destroyed.

By this time it was half-past two o-clock in the morning. The sight of the burning city when the conflagration was at its height, was appalling. A roaring, tossing sea of fire, its waves at intervals leaping high into the air, as one great building after another collapsed, lighting up the country all around, and the thick smoke canopy overhead; the crackling of burning beams; the crash of falling roofs, the roaring of the wind, now increased to a gale; the fierce heat and suffocating smoke; the terror-stricken inhabitants flying before the destroyer, trying to save some wrecks of their furniture and household goods; the cries of weeping women, hurrying with their children to places of safety—all constituted a scene which not even the pen of a Dante could describe.

The next morning I took a walk around the awful scene of devastation. It was heart-rending. Nothing visible for a mile from Devon Row but chimneys and fallen or tottering walls. The thick smoke, from the smouldering ruins, still filled the air. Where yesterday stood the homes of fifteen thousand people, there were only ashes and *debris*, or walls and chimney-stalks, ghastly in their nakedness. The wrecks of the fanes of religion stood out, then broken walls pointing heavenward, as if in mournful protest against the desecration that had been wrought.

And the poor inhabitants, where were they? It made the heart ache to see the groups of men, women, and children, with weary, blood-shot eyes and smoke-begrimed faces, standing over their scraps of furniture and clothing—some of them asleep on the ground from utter exhaustion,—all with despondency depicted on their faces. They filled the park and grounds around the city. Many hundreds escaped with nothing but the clothes they wore; others had caught up some small wrecks of their property. They had no shelter for their heads, and in many cases had lost all. At least twelve thousand people were burnt out. The value of the proper-

A discouraging scene of Water Street stores.

ty destroyed is estimated at from fifteen to twenty millions of dollars, of which about one-third is covered by insurance. The middle class are the greatest sufferers. Hundreds of families, from comfort and independence, are now brought to penury, and have to begin life afresh. The burnt area is a mile in length, and from a quarter to half a mile in breadth, being more than two-thirds of the city, and that by far the better portion.

St. John's has received a terrible blow, and of course it will affect the whole colony and its trade and industries. The fire of 1846 was not to be compared with this in regard to the value of the property destroyed. The city had made very great progress within the past thirty-five or forty years. I had watched its advance with pride and pleasure during that time, and admired the energy and industry of its noble-hearted people. Now I gaze sadly on the wreck of the results of forty years of toil and endeavor—of civilization and progress.

But St. John's will rise from its ashes, improved and beautified, I hope, but not in my day. Help has come from all quarters, liberal, generous, sympathetic. As after the fire of 1846, Boston has contributed generously for the relief of the sufferers. All the great cities of the United States and Canada are sending aid. Our people are taking courage, after the first shock, and already the sound of hammer and axe in rebuilding is heard on all hands. There will soon be plenty of work and good wages. There is no weak despondency. "A stout heart to a stae brae" is the watchword. We have serious difficulties to face, but with hope and courage we can surmount them. Meantime, I would say, we need all possible help.

M. HARVEY

St. John's, Oct. 1, 1892

The ruins of what was once a beautiful church at the foot of Cathedral Street.

Hope Through The Flame
On the St. John's Fire of 1892.

Once more, O City, by new grief laid low,
A brand, fierce burning, writes they lurid name,
Linking the letters with the fiery woe—
Thy limbs are smitten by relentless foe,
Thy life once more afflicted by the Flame!
Again from smouldering homes that toil had given
Is heard the plaintive chant by Sorrow sung,
From hardy children by diaster driven—
Once cheery natures now in spirit riven—
The wail, the song of ringing want is wrung.
Lone Isle, bereaved like chosen race of old,
Heaven sure reserves for thee some dear desire—
Some cherished stamp designs, of choice untold,
To form thy value as of chastened gold,
So cruel tried in crucible of fire!
E'en now as Fate thy cup of sadness fills
The blaze that vital fuel there consumes
Each heart with thought of filial purpose thrills,
Becomes a love-lit beacon on thy hills,
And vision of thy sons far-off illumes.
O Motherland who breasts the striving sea,
Bid thy brave sons gird up their loins as men,
Bestir their hearts in new-found strength for thee—
Through storm of flame or flood arise, and be
Maternal soil of hope and sturdy soul again!
Henry O'Meara.
Boston, October, 1892.

A great deal of manual labour was required to clean up after the fire. Shown here on the right is O'Brien Brothers, one of the few businesses remaining intact.

Through St. John's Fire

A Bostonian's Description of the Calamity.

We left Halifax for St. John's, N.F., on Monday, July 4, arriving in the latter place at eight o'clock, Wednesday morning. We put up at the Central, and, the house being full, had to take quarters on the third floor.

Friday afternoon, between four and five o'clock, we heard the fire-bells ringing, and saw a cloud of smoke rising from a place apparently half a mile away from the hotel. We had been invited to take tea with friends at the East end of the city, and our host, arriving about six o'clock with his carriage, took us to his fine residence on the hill, about a mile or so from our hotel. As we drove along, our minds began to misgive us, seeing that the wind was blowing fiercely, and the flames striding onward in the direction of the Central.

Our window at the table of our host overlooked the whole city, and we soon found that it would be advisable to hasten to our luggage, if we would save it, for it had become evident to all that the city would be swept by the flames to the water's edge. Our party of four accordingly started for the hotel, the youngest, a lady, keeping well ahead of the others, remembering that the trunks were unpacked, and that we were on the third floor.

When we arrived within a few hundred yards of the house we found the Court-House (nearly opposite) a sheet of flames, the woodwork flying in great "flankers" across the street. The entrance to the house was blocked with the luggage of the boarders who happened to be near enough to reach the place, and with the utmost difficulty we reached our rooms, now literally walled in by fire—a large store below us having burst out into roaring flames.

Hastily thrusting our things into trunks and bags, we started over the stairs, dragging what we could. Reaching the street, we found it comparatively clear, the heat and the danger having driven away those who were standing there when we went up.

The Central Hotel, from which our Bostonian friend was forced to flee after having checked in only a few hours before.

A boy or a man whom we might impress into our service would stay a very brief space, as the shillings were freely offered for a "lift"; but by dint of dragging and carrying we got what we had with us along a quarter of a mile or so, and rested. Our host of the evening, seeing one of his men in the crowd, hailed him, and a hand-cart and willing hands soon put us under our friend's roof, with the greater part of our luggage saved.

Those of the family who were familiar with the streets were out all night doing what they could to save their own, and, when that was impossible, helping those whom it was possible to help in saving their property; while we who were unfamiliar with the old city, could only gaze on at a safe distance, and grieve to see such awful destruction.

Imagine a sea of fire more than half a mile wide sweeping along with a terrific roar, taking everything in its course of a mile to the wharves and docks. Immense pieces of fire flying in advance of the main body, like carriers or pickets, set a dozen fires ahead of it, leaping into flames long distances away, forming a skirmish line on and on, until the docks were reached.

The cries of those on the outskirts were: "There goes the English Cathedral!" (a magnificent building costing between $500,000 and $600,000). "There goes St. Patrick's Hall!" "There goes the Kirk!" "Masonic Hall!" "Total Abstinence Hall!" and so on all through the night.

Never did such a pyrotechnic display meet the eyes of any of our party.

When daylight came we walked as far as we could through the ruins, and penetrated to within sight of our hotel. The end walls of stone and the chimneys were still standing, and the coal was burning in the basement; all else had vanished in highly rarefied air.

The Court-House, near by, in which one of our party had spent an hour in chat with sub-Sheriff Chauncey, his friend of twenty-five years ago, and whom he had not seen for that length of time, had neither bench to sit on nor bar to be brought to. Even the royal motto, which he had noticed, with a period after each word, thus, "Dieu. et. Mon. Droit.," had come to a full stop after so many years of looking down upon the prisoner at the bar, who could claim under it his rights.

We remained in St. John's till 10 o'clock A.M., and the sights we saw were indeed pitiful. Every available vehicle had been obtained, and what was saved was being carted to the fields and the places of shelter round the city. The poor, with the commonest of things in their hands, and those better off, with the choicest, were on the streets, some having a definite object in view, some knowing not where to turn.

At 1:30 Saturday morning, while we were watching the singular aspect of the flame in the tower of the Scotch church, a man came to the door of our host and said, "The Minister of the Kirk wants to secure your vacant house." The little gardens on the hill behind the fire were filled with such things as were saved—upright pianos, cook stoves, broken china, etc.

But as we had planned to go to Harbor Grace, we concluded to leave St. John's by the 10 o'clock train. On the way to the depot, when we saw an acquaintance, it was "Did you save anything?"—"Yes, my books."—"What I have on."—"Nothing."—"We got the vessel into the stream, and we're all right," etc.

On the train were those who had friends along the railroad (one hundred to Harbor Grace). Among the passengers was a baby six weeks old, with nurse and maid. The maid said they saved the wedding silver of two years ago, and little else.

We had started for Harbor Grace, but were destined to other experiences before we could reach the desired haven. The weather had been exceedingly dry for a month or more—not a shower of any account in that time. Before we reached Topsail, twelve miles out, we could see that the country was all ablaze with forest fires, and the farther we pushed on the worse it grew. Our train was due in Harbor Grace at 3.30. At 1 o'clock we reached Holyrood; at 1.35 Salmon Cove, through fire and smoke almost blinding; at 2 o'clock a station a little farther on.

After a short delay we try another little piece, halting to get fresh air in the gaps between the flames, and then again dashing through. Then we came to a sea of surging flames, and the word is, "Back to Salmon Cove!" And back we go miles and miles through the burning woods.

We raided the refreshment rooms, and crackers and beer being the staple articles there, we get back to our car with such food.

After an hour's rest we again go on, passing a small station or two, and perhaps a few miles beyond where we had once before been; but suddenly we meet a wall of flame that it is impossible to pass through, and the order is "Back to Salmon Cove!" This is no easy matter, but we finally get there, passing by the flaming ruins of a lumber mill that was standing unhurt when we went on a few minutes earlier. But even Salmon Cove was too warm for us, and the order was, "Back to Holyrood!"

And there we stayed in Holyrood, like the Israelites of old, with a pillar of fire on one side of us and the green sea of the ocean on the other, till 8.30, until the roadmaster came on from St. John's in another train, and, taking charge, pushed us on again toward Salmon Cove and Harbor Grace.

We meet a train at Whitbourne with people going back to find their families, and with cooked provisions for the homeless ones, and we arrive in Harbor Grace at 1.30 Sunday morning, ten hours late. Even at that hour, and in the outskirts of the town, where the station is, one thousand people are awaiting the coming of the train. Harbor Grace station probably never before saw such a crowd.

This is all that was left of the once beautiful and stately Church of England Cathedral. Several men in the picture are viewing the ruins.

Episcopal Cathedral

The Episcopal, or English Cathedral, as it was called in St. John's, a view of which appears in this SOUVENIR, was built from plans furnished by the late SIR GILBERT SCOTT, the most eminent English architect of the present era. It was conceded to be the finest piece of Gothic architecture in the New World. In fact, it was a perfect gem. The lofty proportions of the interior and the fine Gothic colonnades of stone between the nave and the aisles, together with the high lancet-windows, formed a pleasant picture. The carving on the pulpit, pews, and lectern was the admiration of all tourists who visited the Cathedral. The edifice was 120 feet in length and 56 feet broad, and a large portion of the stone used in its erection was imported from Europe. The foundation-stone was laid in 1843 by BISHOP AUBREY S. SPENCER. Bishop Spencer was succeeded in 1844 by DR. EDWARD FEILD, who continued Bishop for thirty-two years, and during his life the construction of the Cathedral was pushed along. Bishop Feild died in 1876, and was succeeded by his coadjutor, DR. J.B. KELLY, who resigned, owing to ill health, in 1877. He was succeeded in 1878 by the REV. LLEWELLYN JONES, D.D., the present Episcopalian bishop, who, with the deepest sorrow, witnessed its destruction on the 8th of July, 1892.

The engraving of the Cathedral, also the scenes before and after the fire, in this SOUVENIR, are from photographs made by S.H. PARSONS, ESQ., St. John's, Newfoundland.

Comments on the Fire

Some four months ago the Eastern Division of the town of St. John's was suddenly reduced to ashes, and to-day nothing remains to mark the sites where the homes of ten thousand people stood and the monuments of the piety and benevolence of its citizens were erected than a wilderness of chimneys and a heap of unsightly ruins. The actual horror of the night of the 8th of July is past to the people of St. John's. But they have yet to face an actuality which is sufficiently serious to contemplate. Relieved from the imminent dread of immediate destruction, it becomes their duty now to relieve disaster, and, if possible, to turn even their troubles to good account. They have lost a city; let the world see if they cannot erect a better one on its site. The opportunity is clearly afforded them, for the fire has swept all obstacles from their path. The only question is, then, whether or not they have the means. This question, we think, may be answered affirmatively. It is worth some trouble to revive St. John's. Situated on the side of a hill that slopes steeply and evenly enough to make its drainage a simple matter, it is yet not too steep for traffic, provided the streets are carried along the proper grade. At the base of the town lies a harbor that for its size approaches as nearly as possible to perfection. One source of trouble only stands in the way. The absentee landlord is at this moment as much an impediment to municipal reform as he has hitherto been to commercial enterprise. The time is now come to deal with him as they would deal with any other obstacle in the way of their progress. Is it not possible to devise a scheme for removing him—first, however, compensating him for the losses that may be inflicted. That compensation should be reasonable, but it certainly should not err on the side of extravagance. By removing the absentee the town becomes the citizens own; and then let them make the best they can of their newly acquired freehold.

Buildings Destroyed.

The following is a pretty correct list of the number of buildings destroyed by the great fire at St. John's on the 8th and 9th July, 1892. There are a few localities where the returns were uncertain, and consequently are not given in this table; namely, Signal Hill, Carter's Hill East, Nunnery Hill, and Bell Chute:

Gower Street, South	136
Gower Street, North	103
Queen's Road, South	42
Queen's Road, North	32
Darling Street, North	22
Darling Street, South	17
Chapel Street	4
Victoria Street, West	23
Victoria Street, East	27
Cathedral Street	15
Cathedral Street, West	4
Long's Hill, West	29
Long's Hill, South	8
Long's Hill, North	8
Long's Lane	19
Livingstone Street	25
Allan's Square	19
Balsam Street	15
Cathedral Hill	12
Dicks Square	14
Bell Street	13
Bulley's Lane	19
Harvey Street	24
Chapel Lane	5
Boggan's Lane	20
Beck's Cove	7
Carter's Hill, West	25
Carter's Hill, East	-
Cookstown	35
Custom House Hill	1
Gambier Street	3
Holloway Street	5
Gregory's Lane	1
Merchant's Lane	1
McBride's Hill	5

Goodview Street	23
Cochrane Street	55
Military Road	13
Bond Street	19
Bannerman Street, West	6
Bannerman Street, East	10
Colonial Street, East	12
Colonial Street, West	6
Quidi Vidi Road	-
Signal Hill Road	-
Ordnance Square	16
Duke York Street	9
King's Road	61
Prescott Street	75
British Square	20
Flavin's Lane	20
Carey Street	10
Nunnery Hill	30
Ryland Place	9
Covel Lane	6
Kickham's Lane	12
Pilots Hill	14
Garrison Hill	17
LeMarchant Road	11
Young Street	-
Freshwater Road	7
Water Street, South	83
Water Street, North	121
Duckworth Street, South	73
Duckworth Street, North	92
Total number of houses burned	1,572

Description of the City of St. John's

This is a description of the city as it was previous to the great fire:

St. John's is the capital and commercial metropolis of Newfoundland. The population in 1884 was 28,610. (It is safe to say that at the time of the great fire it was 30,000.)

The site of the city ascends gradually from the harbor, the highest point being two hundred and twenty-five feet above the sea. It is built on the north side of the harbor.

The principal street is Water Street, running parallel to the north side of the harbor, somewhat more than a mile and a half in length, containing well-constructed houses and large and substantial stores; excellent wharves jut into the water, and vessels of large tonnage can at all times safely moor at them.

The houses and stores of Water Street are built of brick or stone, a law to that effect having been passed after the disastrous fire of 1846, by which the greater part of the city was destroyed.

The houses in the other streets, for the most part, are built of wood.

The Roman Catholic Cathedral stands on the highest point of the declivity which forms the site of the city, two hundred and twenty-five feet above sea level. Opposite the city, at the south side of the harbor, a lofty ridge of precipitous hills, seven hundred feet high, rises abruptly from the water's edge, and stretches for some miles into the interior. A small space at the base of these hills has been made available for building, and here the merchants have erected warehouses and large vats for the manufacture and storing of oil.

The city is well supplied with water from a lake called Twenty-Mile Pond, distant six miles, and elevated one hundred and fifty feet above the highest part of St. John's.

(It is this fact that gave the inhabitants such confidence in the oft-repeated assertion that their city could never be destroyed by fire.) The water-works were constructed at a cost of £80,000 sterling. There are two organized volunteer fire companies.

There are three banks.

There are ten churches in the city. The Roman Catholic Cathedral is an imposing structure. The Church of England Cathedral is also a fine edifice, in fact a gem in Gothic architecture. There are three Wesleyan churches, one Presbyterian church, three Church of England, and three Roman Catholic churches, and one Congregational church.

The most important public edifices, in addition to the Cathedrals and churches, are: Government House, the residence of the governor, a plain but substantial and commodious stone building, which cost £30,000 sterling when erected in 1822; the House of Assembly, in which the Legislature holds its sittings and where are the government offices; the Union and Commercial banks; the Lunatic Asylum; the Public Hospital, Market-house, and Court-House; Roman Catholic college and convents; Episcopalian, Wesleyan, and General Protestant academies; Roman Catholic and Episcopalian orphan asylums; the Athenaeum; St. Patrick's Hall; Star of the Sea Hall; Total Abstinence Hall.

Eighteen life, fire, and marine insurance companies have agencies in St. John's.

The joint stock companies are: The St. John's Gas Light Company, General Water Company, Floating Dry Dock Company, Colonial Cordage Company, Boot & Shoe Facer Company, St. John's Steam Tug Company.

The city has two saw mills, two furniture factories, two machine shops, one gas manufactory, three iron foundries, one distillery, two breweries, four bakeries by machinery, one patent slip, one floating dock, one tannery, one boot and shoe factory, two tobacco factories, one soap and candle works, one rope, twine, and net factory.

Of the literary institutions, the St. John's Athenaeum has a library containing 7,000 volumes, and a reading-room well supplied with British and American newspapers and periodicals; the Academy has a reading-room and library, and the City and Metropolitan Clubs have reading-rooms.

The newspapers published in St. John's are the "Daily Evening Telegram," "Daily Evening Colonist," and the "Daily Evening Herald;" the "Advocate," tri-weekly; the "Newfoundlanders," and the "Times," bi-weekly; the "Patriot," and the "Royal Gazette," weekly. Of these newspapers, the "Royal Gazette" is the oldest, having been established in 1806.

The large mercantile establishments issue supplies on a large scale for the prosecution of the seal and cod fisheries and collect and export fish and oil. The codfish are chiefly sent to Great Britain, Spain, Portugal, Italy, the West Indies, and Brazil. The seal oil and the seal skins are mainly exported to Britain.

The great bulk of the imports of the colony arrives at the port of St. John's.

In addition to the large mercantile establishments there are a large number of handsome retail shops.

The average number of vessels entering the port annually is 1,500, having a burden of 270,000 tons. The number of sailing-vessels clearing from port for the seal fisheries each year was once very great, but of late years these have been largely superseded by steamers. Eighteen powerful steamers now leave St. John's each year for the seal fishery March 10, or soon after.

List of Contributors.

Collected by messrs. Stratton, Little, & Co., and Edw. T. Russell, Esq.

Nash, Spaulding, & Co.	$1,000.00
E.T. Russell & Co.	250.00
W.A. Wood & Co.	200.00
Dana Hardware & Co.	200.00
John D. & M. Williams	200.00
Stratton & Little	200.00
Jordan, Marsh, & Co.	200.00
Brown, Durrell, & Co.	200.00
Maverick Oil Company	200.00
Holmes & Nichols	200.00
Directors of Manf. Nat. Bank	100.00
Whitney, Pousland, & Co.	100.00
Acme Extract Company	100.00
Thos. J. Whidden	100.00
Gloucester Net & Twine Co.	100.00
N. Boynton & Co.	.50.00
Glover & Wilcomb	.50.00
John Porteous	.10.00
From Cambridge Committee	624.05
American Net & Twine Company, Ivers W. Adams, Treas.	500.00
Brockton Committee	278.55
Kidder, Peabody, & Co.	250.00
William K. Vanderbilt	250.00
From Lynn Committee	231.00
Boston Terra-Novian Association	200.00
Jas. A. St. John	110.00
Boston Herald	100.00
Boston Globe	100.00
Joseph S. Pray	100.00
James J. Grace	100.00
A.W. Spencer	100.00
Shepard, Norwell, & Co.	100.00
Walter Johnston	100.00
Reiter & Co., Highland Spring Brewery	100.00
Newfoundlandrs' Mutual Benefit Association	100.00
Henry Bevins	100.00
Shepard Brooks	100.00
Theodore Lyman	100.00
Jos. S. Fay	100.00

The Transcript Company	100.00
Joseph B. Glover	100.00
Ames Plow Company	100.00
J.D.W.	100.00
W.G. Means	100.00
Jos. S. Pray	100.00
A.W. Spenser	100.00
H.M. Whitney	100.00
Daniel Lawrence & Son	100.00
Francis C. Foster	100.00
Boston Type Foundry	.50.00
John R. Alley	.50.00
Parkinson & Burr	.50.00
Houghton, Mifflin, & Co.	.50.00
Bell Telephone Company, John E. Hudson, Treasurer	.50.00
Wm. J. Emerson	.50.00
B. Schlessinger	.50.00
Jonathan A. Lane	.50.00
R.J. Todd	.20.00
John W. O'Ryan	.20.00
Mrs. J. Armory Davis	.20.00
Milville Committee	.17.50
Collected by Enoch Piccott, and paid in St. John's	.16.97
Rev. Denis O'Callaghan	.15.00
Edward N. Perkins	.15.00
Prof. H.W. Forrey	.15.00
A. Friend	.15.00
Isaac McLean	.15.00
Prof. H.W. Torrey	.15.00
Friends in Bradley Building	.10.25
First Baptist Mariners' Church	.10.17
Arthur Searle	.10.00
Williamn Read	.10.00
Hon. John Read	.10.00
E.B. James	.10.00
William E. Doyle	.10.00
H.E. Scudder	.10.00
Henry C. Carrick	.10.00
Collected by J.H. Dalton	.10.00
David H. Fitzgerald	.10.00
Dr. H.O. Marcy	.10.00
Rev. A.A. Miner	.10.00
H. Libby & Son	.10.00

Rockwell & Churchill	10.00
Hon. A.B. Alger	10.00
Rebecca M. Smith	10.00
George W. Gay, M.D.	10.00
James Hodder	10.00
Robert Levi	10.00
C. Lowell	10.00
A. Robinson & Co.	10.00
Jacob Morse	10.00
James Stitson	10.00
John Walsh	10.00
E.M. Phelan	10.00
Cash	10.00
B.S.	50.00
Hon. William Taylor	50.00
Dr. John F. Couch	50.00
From sundry parties	47.00
Employees A. Stowell	32.50
S.B. Yerxa	30.00
Temple St. M.E. Church	28.00
John Turner, Rhode Island	25.00
A.F. Estabrook	25.00
Morse Bros.	25.00
A. Friend, J.A.W.	25.00
Nova Scotian	25.00
A.B. Martin	25.00
Luther S. Johnson & Co., Lynn	25.00
Felton & Son	25.00
William Johnson & Co.	25.00
Hon. M.M. Cunniff	25.00
J.K. Souther & Son	25.00
James W. Kennedy	25.00
Hon. Owen A. Galvin	25.00
J.A. White	25.00
Chase, Parker, & Co.	25.00
Dr. John G. Lane	25.00
J.B. Hand	25.00
James A. Kennedy	25.00
A.M. Ward & Co.	25.00
Carpenter, Woodward, & Morton	25.00
Thomas Frye	25.00
John T. Kennedy	25.00
A. Stowell	25.00
A.M. Ward Company	25.00
John P. Squire	25.00

Joseph G. Gallishaw	.23.00
Stephen O'Meara	.20.00
W.R. Driver	.20.00
F.J. Child	.20.00
John G. Pike	.20.00
Edward H. Allen	.20.00
S.J. Donovan	.10.00
Wm. McDonald	.10.00
John C. Crowley	.10.00
Nicholas J. Ryan	.10.00
A. Friend	.10.00
L.W. Scott & Co.	.10.00
Dr. T.C. Barden	.10.00
S.J. Denning	.10.00
Michael J. Moore	.10.00
A. Robinson & Co.	.10.00
Habich & Co.	.10.00
Thomas Burke	.10.00
Joseph Hancock	.10.00
Mrs. A.H. Gallagher	.10.00
Rev. M.H. Kittredge	.10.00
John T. Rawlins	.10.00
Thomas Mulloy	.10.00
R.J. Druhan	.10.00
William Whittle	.10.00
Michael J. Carey	.10.00
John T. Renison	.10.00
J.C. Collins	.10.00
Local Assembly, K. of L., No. 5789	.10.00
R.R. Walsh	.10.00
Henry D. Winton	.10.00
Rev. John O'Brien	.10.00
Rev. Francis Butler	.10.00
Goepper Bros.	.10.00
John O'Day	.10.00
Simon Walsh	.10.00
Richard McCormick, Two Harbors, Minn.	.10.00
J.P. McCormick	.10.00
J.T. McCarthy	7.50
Employees Howard Iron Foundry	6.50
Mrs. W.B. Berry	6.00
Mrs. W.B. Berry	6.00
E.E. Chain, Treasurer, St. John's M.E. Church	6.00
"Friends"	5.70

Duckworth Street just east of the Courthouse, near the foot of Church Hill. Every piece of debris had to be removed by hand, as there were no mechanical means available ... a monumental task.

The following-named persons contributed $5.00:

J. Deason, J.J. O'Connor, Dr. Howard, St. Margaret's Church, Chas. M. DeMeritt, Elliott J. Hyde, W.F. Habock, Albert H. Roffy, H.J. Ross, J.F. Powers, W. Taylor, Jr., Albert Barlow, Andrew C. Hughes, Matthew Coady, John J. Rowe, Richard Kelly, J.L. Johnston, R.G. Southworth, W.B. Wilner, Mary Cashin, Robert Chauncey, F.H. Mudge, T.J. White, Evin Morden & Co., H.W. Dean, Capt. C.J. Moore, Edward Brien, Barclay, Clements, & Co., Riding & Co., Jas. J. Lawlor, B.W. Johnston, William E. O'Flaherty, Mrs. W.H. Peterson, John Laracy, Quinsler & Co., Mrs. McMorrow, Touy Bros. & Co., Michael McCarthy, John O'Neil, W.J. Higgins, W. Broderick, Bernard Devine, John P. Wise, Thos. F. Lannen, G.N. McGuire, Capt. G.F.H. Murray, Thos. N. Brown, Thos. F. Kevin, Geo. J. Sutton, Standard Clothing Co., J.F. & W.H. Falvey, Peoples' Clothing Store, Pierce McCarthy, Edward Pynn, P.W. Coleman, C.H. Brown, P.J. Mansfield, E.G. Taylor, M.J. Corliss, Broadway Clothing Co., P.B. Corbett, Thos. B. Fitz, Dr. M.W. O'Keefe, Patrick Bonia, P.J. Kavanaugh, J.L. Fitzgerald, A. Stowell, Patsey Sheppard, Thos. W. Norman, John G.R. Smith, P.J. Renison, E. Prescott, Robert Canning, P.J. Feehan, Thos. Higgins, Wm. Fitzgerald, Wm. Mountain, Wm. Smith & Co., F.S. Green, P. Hayes, Wood Bros. Pomeroy & Fisher, Joseph Joyce, T.R. Tarrant, Sanford F. Petts, Henry Gallishaw, M. Barr, E.S. Booth, Thos. W. Acouct, W. Devanna, Mark Phillips, J.J. Reardon, T.P. Ryan, Mrs. F. Hyde, J.T. Conner, M. & E. Ryan, Mrs. C.D. Raynes, Peter Rielley, Miss M.M. Dowsley, Miss A.M. Dowsley, A Friend, J.F. Merrill, L.J. Logan, Mr. Dierkes, Mrs. Mary Winn, Hugh Devine, James Stack, Mr. Heard, Brockton; J. Barron, Dr. James J. Putnam, M.A. Boland, John Burns, B.S. Snow, J.R. Neal, N.B. Freeman, Charles Miller, Rev. J.J. McNulty, "Christian Endevor," John McNulty, Dr. A.W. Howard, S.H. Winkley, Dr. H.W. Emerson, William Cash, J.J. McAuliffe, John LaRoche, D.W. Gage, Samuel A. Hopkins, M.D., M.E. Ellis, James J. Putnam, Mrs. H. Squire, A.F.S. E.F. Donohoe, Cleveland, Ohio;—Boynton, Arrin M. Lowe, Henry O'Meara, F.A.H., Jabez B. Cole, H. John Burns & Co., B.B. Snow & Co., J.R. Wall & Co., Conquest & Hodgkins,

A.F. Rich & Co., Gloucester Fish Co., P.J. O'Hara & Co., Col. T.W. Higginson, Mrs. Emeline Ellis.

Not Classified under any heading

Michael Parrell, $4.00; Jas. Devine, $4; Friends, $4.05; Friends, $3.10; Friends, $3.85; Miss Grace Maddan, $4; D.J. Lewis, $2.50; W. Halligan, $2.50; W.H. Ash, $2.50; J.H. Dalton, $2.50; John Hally, $1.50; Moses Furniss, $1.50; A Friend, 75 cts; Thos. Noseworthy, $1.50; John Foley, $1.50; John Magner, 75 cts; J. McNamara, 75 cts; Robert Wiseman, 75 cts; A Friend, 35 cts; J. Kinney, 35 cts; P. Baldwin, 35 cts; A Friend, 15 cuts; Mr. Broderick, 65 cts; M. Young, 5 cts; Mrs. Gollastien, 15 cts; W. Cohen, 15 cts.

The following-named persons contributed $3.00 each:

Michael Hingey, John Conway, Mrs. M.J. Haines, D.F. Bradley, A Friend, C.W. Davis, W.A. Snow & Co., Barber Bros., E.M. Messenger, M.F. Morrissey; David Henry, M.F. Quinn, B. Gearidge, Miss A. Byrne, J.H. Mullane, Geo. Walker, Ed. Gardner, Esther Brien, Frank Burke, William Johnston, Jas. L. Jordan, Mary A. Gavin, Palmer & Co., Abe Gallishaw, Miss Lucy O'Connor, Wm. J. Burke, B.J. Short, William Johnson, F.E. Meaney, Conquest & Hodgkins, Mary and Annie Manning, Thomas Snow, Snow & Rich, Joseph Furlong.

The following-named persons contributed $2.00 each:

John Stapleton, James Rieley, John Hancock, Martin M. Christopher, Patrick Mountain, William Mountain, Jr., S. Waddleton, Jas. Wilcox, Peter Kelly, Miss E. Hagerty, Chas. Dutton, Michael Green, P.J. Kent, P.O'Gara, W.H. Gorden, Richard Flemming, Ed. Davis, P.J. Brazil, P.T. Morrissey, H. Bloomfield, Mr. Cross, Edger & Co., Patrick Rielly, Wm. Mallard, Wm.

McEvoy, C.E. Osgood, J. Cohen, Isaac Walker, John H. Lee, Chas. W. Sanderson, J.A. Hathaway, Geo B. Levernon, Osburn Haws, Aug. Pume, James Kennedy, Jas. O'Meara, H.A. Holden, E.W. Clives, John Doody, Annie Fow, Thos. Arthur, Annie T. Kennedy, John McWeeney, P.B. McManus, Kennedy & Quigley, Mrs. Walsh, M. Morrissey, David Walsh, C.S. Johnson, C.A. Clapp, Andrew Porter, Geo. Marshall, Billings B. Reed, Mrs. P.J. Mansfield, Mr. Harmondi, A.L. Marsh, F. Dunphy, Miss Maggie Dunn, John F. Kirby, Edward Gagand, A Friend, J.B. Halleran, Bremner & Co., P. Higgins, John Ellis, An Irishman, Frank P. Ford, Thos. F. Harden, J.W. Buckley, Dr. W.H. Devine, Fannie Walsh, M.J. Corless, Thos. J. Pierson, J.J. McNamara, J.J. Cousins, Edward L. Cousins, Geo. H. Harris, S.A. Give, Thos. Butler & Co., John Burnes, P. Quigley, L.T. Pratt & Co., P.A. Sheehan, Jos. Forsyth, Frank Forsyth, A Friend, John Carty, Delton C. Grimes, Geo. Donovon, M.J. Chambers, M.D. Emerson, F.A. Hubbard, P.F. Carroll, J.E. Briston, Cash, P.A. Murray, S.M. Wright, Thos. Fitzgerald, A Friend, Thos. Brien, A Friend, G.W. Mason, Howard K. Foster, W. Stoddard, F.J. Flynn, C.P. Donohoe, J.J. Roache, M.J. Murphy, Alphonsas Croak. F. Furlong, R. Joy, E.A. Knight, P.J. Grace, J.F. O'-Donnell, A Friend, Cornelius Hurley, M.J. Renison, Gilber Pynn, B. White, Thos. White, Peter Duchemin, M.M. Breen, Miss Ellen Druhan, Wm. Lynch, Robert Ford, H.P. McDermott, L.H. Sullivan, Catherine Murray, James Roberts, David Tilley, Lambert Bros. Annie Rielly, Jay Street, Berlin, N.H.; Daniel Kiely, L.C. Crowley, Foley & Crook, Walter Walsh, C.M. Guetts, Henry Flynn, R. M. Kelly, Gloucester Fish Co., Baker & Witherall, E.A. Rich, P.H. Prior, O.H. Willy, Laylor & Mayo, Wright Bros. Patrick Harper, Mrs. E.P. Lanelle, John Meaney, Mrs. J. Connelly, Dr. E.F. Boland, C.H. St. John, Geo. Eddy, A Friend, A Friend, Thomas Marden, I. Street, Atwood & Co., M.F. Blanchard, Freeman & Cobb, Baker, Witherall & Co., Rich & Storey, Taylor, Mayor, N.D. Freeman & Co., Arnold & Winsor, Lambard & Curtis, P.H. Puir, Paris, Ingalls & Co., C. Hunt & Co., N.J. Sullivan, Rich Bros. Story & Stevens, Peckins & Bates, S.J. Jackson, Blanchard & Towle, J. Roche & Co., J.E. Jiles, R.M. Kelly, Joseph House, Mrs. M. Culverwell.

The following-named persons contributed $1.00 each:

James Lahey, F. Bousquet, J.M. Robie, Isaac Slocum, O.E. Pierce, A Friend, Harry Hall, Mrs. J. Smart, W.H. Stafford, W. Leggett, L.J. Tobin, D. Sullivan, Jas. Hodden, W. J. Asmond, Geo. Mells, Geo. S. Linfield, Walter Hawkins, John Young, Noah Nober, Isaac Linfield, Robert Boyd, Denis Power, W. Philmore, D. Foley, Mrs. J. Foley, Miss M. O'Leary, Miss K. O'Leary, J.P. Connelly, Mrs. Deacon, Miss E. Toomey, Henry's Hat Store, James Long, E. Shea, Wm. Whelan, James McEvoy, Miss Celia McEvoy, Mr. Woods, Cash, Geo. A. Donagan, Thos. Moore, Patrick Redmond, Mr. Melligan, Peter Hughes, W.C. Cox, C.F. W., P.J. Murphy, J.W.W., James Roache, T.P. Haggerty, James Smart, Richard Mearns, J. Wyzanski, F. Sproules, A Friend, B. Atkinson & Co., Patrick O'Brien, Mrs. Fitzpatrick, Miss McLaughlin, F.H. Casey, Mrs. Margaret Christopher, John Bailey, Mary Bailey, Michael McLaughlin, Mrs. M. McLaughlin, Frank A. Woodbury, John McChrystal, Patrick Shea, Thomas McCarty, John Murphy, G. Fitzpatrick, Robert Rogerson, W.S. Alexander, Frank C. Wood, T.P. Sproule, John Kelly, H.D. Hufgan, Geo. Bussey, B.A. & Co., J.J. Killian, W.J. Donovan, Josephine Pendergast, Daniel Costello, Mrs. M. Griffin, W. Parnell, W. Colleton, John Fortune, Mr. M. Fortune, C.D. Kenefick, Isaac Maddock, Peter Dunphy, Richard Glynn, Joseph Crawford, Thomas Roache, Michael Foley, Thomas Mullaly, Philip Johnson, Robert Yetman, Stephen Meade, Richard Waddleton, John Waddleton, Sen. Patrick Ward, Thos. Rossiter, John Connell, John Powell, Michael Kilkenny, James Delaney, Robert Yetman, Jr., Patrick Yetman, James Coleman, John Mountain, Edward Sweeney, Mrs. M. Mountain, Wm. Kinsella, James Reed, Miss T. Delaney, John Mallowney, Joseph Delaney, John Sheehan, Geo. Jackman, Timothy Ryan, Thomas Ryan, Thomas Armstrong, John O'Neil, Robert Powell, H. Hammond, Denis Curran, A Friend, Geo. H. Baleterson, Fred Neil, G.S. Swane, W.B.Y., Denis O'Neil, E.J. McCarthy, M.J. Harrington, S. Sullivan, E. Young, G.H. Day, F.H. Sherman, M.F. Donovan, Geo. W. Roddis, P.J. Goodman, Wm. O'Brien, M. Manning, Patrick Neary, C.E. Maloney, J. O'Neil, C.M. Doherty, D. Breslin, J.J. Cross, H.J. Wagenfield, J.M. Swain, G.E. Hubbard, Denis O'Shea, D.F. Poland, W.H. Lewd,

C. Slack, J.M. Blake, S.W. Brackett, A.B. Pudlan, Cash, F.H. Bowls, F.H. Haynes, Cash, Hugh Farrell, John Slocum, E.S. Kenton, P. O'Neil, Sidney Reed, Alice Kevin, Miss C.R., Miss L. McKenna, Michael Rielly, Patrick Rielly, Michael Shea, F.N. Krivenaan, S. London, Frank S. Moloney, John Singlee, E.L. Brown, W. Greening, Thos. J. Lavery, M.W. O'Keefe, G.R. Monroe, B. Sullivan, F. Murphy, Miss Katie Haven, Miss Annie Haven, Miss Nellie Haven, Miss F.J. Nesbit, Miss F.A. Howe, Miss P. Chabot, D.A. Hunter, Josie Larkin, Michael Sullivan, A. Fitzpatrick, Thos. McCormack, A. Hackett, G. Newling, N. Roache, Tobie English, Mr. Kearns, J. Hagen, J. Geogan, E. Franey, D. Sullivan, C. Olston, P. Doyle, W. Heafs, F.A. Hastings, Lindsey, John H. Kelly, C.W. Burke, Mrs. Graves, John F. Sugrue, Francis Allen, C.W. Lewis, J.Y. Wren, J.J. Leary, S.F. Murphy, John Malone, A Friend, F.H. Conner, A Friend, A Friend. J.H. Troy, J. Taylor, E.S. Haymond, W. O'Shea, D.C. Galvin, Dr. Morris, Andrew Gately, L. Curley, Bessie and Mondie Thompson, James H. Crobay, James Hatton, T. Cribben, Robt. Quilty, J. Malaney, Mrs. G. Clifton, Mrs. J. Kennedy, N. Hines, J.A. Fitzgerald, James Kelly, W.J. Barrett, P. Moley, M.J. Brennan, R. Kelleher, R.T. Richie, A. Richards, A Friend, Robert Owen, Wm. Loftus, Jas. Patrick, H. McLaughlin, J.J. Hall, Stephen Smith, Wm. J. Cunninghamn, E.A. Sherman, Emory Hoar, B.Y. Mitchell, P.J. Syme, Cash, Jas. McPherson, W.F.G., F.M.A. Downey, Bruce Ware, C.B. Coffin, Maggie T. Martin, J.N. Bacon, G.H. Morgan, G. P. Atkins, John J.C., "W.F.H.," Cash, Mrs. Whiteway, Wm. Finn, John Wearls, A Friend, Mrs. Franey, A Friend, Sallie A. McGrath, Cash, P.H. O'Brien, A.G. Furnim, J.B. Murphy, Cash, W.H. Ryan, F.H. Harrington, W. Bennett, W.R. Cook, R.D. Coileg, John Mulcahy, A.B. Dunham, G.A. Neaugram, L.O. Robbins, Lambert Chafe, P.B. Hitton, Chas. Moore, John Morrissey, Michael Keough, A Friend, J.P. Martin, T. Sullivan, W. Hickey, James Johnson, Martin Foley, Ricahrd Lawson, Joe Christie, Mrs. B. Christie, W. Forsyth, Mr. Keough, H. Millgan, W. McGrath, S. Butler, G.A. Hosely, E. Powers, L.C. Mackey, M. Donovan, John J. Doyle, G.Ed S. Davis, E.A. Plummer, F. McWiggin, T. Gooman, J. Horton, Mary Boland, J.O. Hyman, W.F. McGluchy, John Brown, Jr., T.L. Brown, J.W. Ross, S. Nehpets, M.L. Streeter, J.P. Mullin, J.E. Histop, W.J. Costello, W.A. Pingree, F.G. Maliff, A.L. Shepard, Alexander T. Brown, John Daley, P.J. Walsh, Minnie Pendergast, Bride Pendergast, Jen-

nie E. Croft, A. Prior, F. Ownes, G.F. Mansfield, Chas. E. Ward, A.M. Dowe, Chas, J. McGeary, Chas. W. Earley, Jas. Smith, J.H. Lauton, M. Keough, A. Dwyer, Chas, Dwyer, L.H. Hanigbaum, Wm. Savage, P. Dunn, J.F. Dooley, F. Mitchell, J. Hedge, John Gunn, A.B. Armstrong, David Plumer, Ira Mosher, John Graham, John O'Brien, A Friend, A Friend, Mrs. M.J. Nugent, D. Sullivan, Geo. A. Morrison, P.F. O'Brien, Cash, Cash, B. Franklin Sanborne, S.W. Hoppe, Mrs. Harding, A Friend, John Tilley, Thos. Kelly, Mrs. Kinsman, John Condon, Thos, Condon, Mary Darichy, Maggie Linton, W. Carey, Miss McMann, Mary Ryan, Mary Ring, Mrs. Lyman, Nellie Barding, Mary Weckler, Mrs. Clifford, J. O'Conner, Covert Bros., W.N. Beary, Timothy W. Hall, John Sheddy, A Friend, A. Geary, A Friend, R. Brien, R.J. Power, D.J. Cantwell, E.J. Erwin & Co., Michael Duggan, P.J. Shea, E.J. Kennedy, Warren Nurse, Hugh Carey, Thos. Seeley, C.A. Noyes, Maggie Field, David Walsh, G.W. Bennis, E.G. Morse, May McElroy, P.J. Touhy, D.J. Madden, F. Sweeney, John McVey, Jos. V. Donahoe, J.B. O'Higgins, Jas. Aspell, M.J. Murphy, Thos. J. Ryan, Richard King, Maurice Foley, Kate Carew, A Friend, F. De Silva, H.A. Fay, M.K. Murphy, R.F. Carew, Richard Kelly, W. Dowley, David Murphy, W. Kelly, John Gardner, E.A. Coan, M.M.B., Mrs. F. O'Conner, D. Govan, J. Hanson, L. O'Brien, Hannah Carthy, P. Doyle, Thos. Roust, James Keefe, Jas. F. Bailey, Miles Foley, John T. Slattery, P.F. Slattery, A Friend, J.D. Southerland, E.J. Dwyer, Thos. Sprules, Timothy McCarthy, A Friend, Thos. Barry, Mr. Canty, D. Westwater, M. Coakley, D. Murry, A Friend, Jennie Keough, John O'Hara, Mrs. Ford, W. Ford, Jas. Jordan, John Kennedy, John Waddleton, L. Hoffman, G.E. John Wilson, J. Deignan, Ellen McCarthy, J. Fitzgerald, Jas. Richards, Maurice Hart, Margaret McCarthy, Edward Wyeatt, Edwart Sullivan, H.A. Hartnett, P.J. Grady, Mrs. K. Murphy, George C. Brennan, Richard Minton, John J. Cotter, Thomas J. Collins, James McCarthy, P. McCarthy, P. Freeman, T.W. Bevan, D. Chapman, E. McClan, John McNeil, Atwood & Co., Cash, Cash, Thomas Callahan, J.M. Donovan, T.W.C., Ellen Manning, David Keefe, William Barry, A Friend, Robert Kershaw, J.L. Spaulding, Jr., R.J.T. Thompson, W.E. Souther, John Souther, Peter Powers, C.J. Scanlan, James J. Green, — Kavanagh, Geo. R. Hardgraves, A.B. Dunham, Chas. A. Wood, M.W. Dooley, Mrs. P. Crowley, J.B. Wiley & Sons, Boston Fish Co., P. Ginness, A. Tarr, J.M. Locher & Co., Thomas Murphy, David J. Keefe, John

Smallcomb, Michael Murphy, Michael Rourke, Frank Gushue, Francis Walsh, Thomas Druhan, Sarah Feehan, Daniel Kean, Peter Conners.

The following-named persons contributed 50 cents each:

A. Main, Neil Duffley, S. Cohen, Jas. Colgan, T. McCarthy, E. Swanahan, J.A.B., W.H.K., J.J.K., E.G.M., W.J. and P., D. McCarthy, E. Marsh, T.M. O'Connell, W.E.H., J.J. Flannigan, W.F. Knowlton, C.W.H., W.F. O'Donnell, H. Devine, B.S. Emsely, B. Belman, C.G. Pond, H.D. Cossett, J. O'Brien, A.D. Brewer. Mr.—, M.E. Doran, S.C. Hay, M.E. Severance, Geo. James, Mrs. Thos. Downey, William Wallace, Mrs. E. Moran, Mary J. Mack, Marguerite Dalay, Maria Campbell, Michael Flynn, W. Higgins, Miss Furze, W.S. Phillips, A.D. Neill, A Friend, A Friend, F.P. Chaplin, S.M., K. Lavin, J. Andrew, Jospeh Wilson, B. Ballagher, J. Crooke, M. Gegley, T. Clavin, N. Mason, Geo. Hall, B. Donnelley, B. Howe, M. Balwin, James Crooke, M.J. Kelly, E. Stafford, P. Rourke, Mr. Howe, P. Moore, M. Coady, D. McCarthy, John O'Brien, D.J.S., H.P. Kittridge, Mrs. M. Tobin, Walter Hart, J.H. Ireland, G.B. Levi, Mrs. Dempsey, Mary Foley, A Friend, J.T.C., R.A. Murray, J.E. Fay, M. Cruith, R. Walsh, Daniel Daley, Edward Sheehan, Peter Gorham, W.H. Hardy, Chas. McCarthy, Chas M. Dogherty, E.L. Rand, A Friend, H. Moriarty, A Friend, A. Wynne, C.H. Morrison, Mary A. Barry, A Friend, A Friend, A Friend, L.J. Sullivan, A Friend, Denis O'Brien, Mrs. McGann, Katie Miliken, Mrs. Keough, John M. Patrigane, M.F. McGrath, Mrs. Ownes, G.W. Bafts. Daniel Flynn, H. Thomas, A Friend, Elsie Des Laurier, Nap. Grise, Roger Gill, J.W. Hutcheson, A.B. Brown, J.V. Finn, Chas. J. Hill, Mr. Coleman, John Purcell, W.C. Merchant, Thomas Rowland, A Friend, Frank Kennedy, John Kellar, James McCarroll, John Bennett, John Diernan, Dan McLane, A Friend, John Powers, Roger Downing, A. Dawe, P.A. Dawe, Samuel Johnson, Edwin Jenesse, Thomas Barry, Owen McEnerney, Sarah Christie, James Feeley, William Walshe, Mrs. Ann Purcill, Walter Kirby, James M. Doyle, Sylvester Maher, James McCuen, James Mulvey, John Corcoran, W.J. Smith, James Molowney, William Brown, James McGovern,

Mrs. McGovern, Thomas Carroll, John Keefe, J. Perry, Mrs. M. Brennan, William Cole, Patrick McCormick, Louise Lynch, P. Miller, J. Crowley, W. Williams, J. Doyle, J. Watts, Mr. Constant, J. Mackay, E. Pears, D. Folks, C. Weldon, W. Hansell, Mr. Nearral, D. Twomey, A. Kronander, Harry Howard, Lucy Pendergast, P. Harrington, Mary Thornton, A. Wood, A.V. Simpson, S.K., T.F. Coughlan, J. Redmond, J.H. Webber, F.H. Dowd, C.H. Abbott, Young—, Hubbard, Colloton & Day, Andrew Granfield, Agnes Kevin, A Friend, J. Brown, A Friend, Miss M. Harvey, John M. Fitzgerald, Frank Haven, M.H. Cohan, Hugh McDevitt, Owen Cunningham, A Friend, M.W. Murphy, J.A. O'Neil, A Friend, Mr. Anderson, T.H. O'Brien, Hugh O'-Conner, A Drummer, G.A.H., G. Burkam, D. Moore, J. Deignon, Oscar C. Anderson, Mr. Swan, Thomas Daly, B. Scott, James Gardner, H. Holland, A Friend, Brook, Andrew Nelson, Friend, T. Marshall, M.F. Butt, W. Megan, A Henrikson, Owen Clary, Frank B. Hamill, Wm. Dalton, Wm. Qualter, John M. Kay, R.T. Qualter, Jas. H. Kenny, Wm. H. Meade, T.E. Rafferty, Mary Croke, E.R. Thorn, M. Dalton, Mrs. M. Dalton, Ed. McKay, R. Neale, John Sullivan, James Duncan, John Duncan, A. Sheater, M. Flavin, James Bowers, J.T. Murphy, T.J. Daly, A Friend.

The following-named persons contributed 25 cents each.

J.M. Herbert, S.E. Ahern, H.R. Ruffee, M.S. Dickinson, J.A.E., G.M. Baker, A.F. King, N.G. Coffee, A.S. Telyea, R.A.C., E. Reddy, J.H. Dale, H.J. Hutchinson, J.S. Johnson, H.J. Waters, J.B. Coken, Mays, Austin, J. Gormley, J.A. McGee, R.C. Harrington, Wm. J. Crowley, Patrick McGurie, P.F. Dunlea, T. Mahoney, John Gaugher, Michael Daley, C.F. Geary, Emil Schilling, Gustave Schilling, Mr. Campbell, M. Davis, A Friend, A Friend, A Friend, A Friend, J. Tooner, F.D. Bayne, W. Lascelles, W. R. Bennett, William Sine, J.M. Coleman, J. Waugh, J. Peacock, W. Barclay, James Acheson, S. Bloaskett, A Friend, Mrs. D. Cotter, P.J. O'Connor, Chas. Caswell, John Matthews, Thomas Dwyer, J. Stewart, E. Devlin, F. Barnice, Thomas H. Foley, J.M. Reando, Geo E. Colley, Gilman C. Dowe, Katie Farreil, Sara Higgins, W. Trickey, Theresa Moriarty, Lizzie

E. Connell, Maggie McLean, Annie Hickey, Nellie Sullivan, Bessie Dooling, K. Shevy. A Friend, C.H. Vorl. Hugh McMartin, T. McGowan, A Black, John J. Walsh, John Manning, Mrs. Parsons, B.R. Christopher, H. Collins, W.E. Young, Michael Tierney, E. Rainey, J. Shong, Wm. Crowley, John Lee, Frank Penders, G.C.K., J.B. Harlow, R. Johnston, Mr. Murphy, Richard Flemming, J. Smith, Gustas Sunberg, Mr. Brennan, Bridget Powell, Ellen Powell, John Hunt, Mrs. Powers, Thomas Heffernan, James Little, M. Kirevin, P. Paterson, John Doyle, D. Flynn, E. Aylward, W. Moran, J. Roach, D. Forrest, J. McDenit, J. O'Connell, C. Lindstal, J. Stabb, H. Morris, J. Luke, L. Holland, W. Halls, J. Stevens, M. Lynch, J. Livingstone, A. Ashley, W. Templeton, J. Hannon. A. Duffy, B. Walsh, J. Walsh, Mr. Mahoney, J. Douglass, D. Mullin, J. Pinckney, D. Geagan, P. Waters, Mr. Dolan, J. Riley, Friend. P. Wall, Mr. Duggan, Mr. Stranger, E. Hagman, R. Walsh, J. Donohue, A. McGinness, C. Hardy, G. Maher, Mr. O'Brien, Mr. Glen, Mr. O'Brien, J. Hickey, G. McLoughlin, F.B. Gray, J.E. Flynn, James Burnes, Mary A. Coffey, John Lavis, B.L. Crooke, Geo. F. Duffy, R.T. Allen, J.H. Andrews, J. Loughead, Peter Kerr, T. Ryan, James Wilson, K. Madden, P. Whalen, A Friend, W.C. Potter, J.F. Kebler, M. O'Brien, P.H.L., A Friend, T. Cashmare, T. Green, T. Driscoll, P.J. Forest, J. Eagan, T. Mullowney, John Leahy, R. Callahan, J. Reagan, Richard Powers, A Friend, M.J. Smart, D. McCarthy, M. Leary, T. Cashman, A Swanson, M.M. Hinsler, L. Harris, H.V. Deihl, Mrs. Walsh, Mrs. E.E. Harvey, F.Y. Oventl, J. Fizley, A Friend, A.C. Hall, J.D. Kenny, C.R. Cox, J.B. Gatkins, Jas. J. Collins, J.F. Logan, M.C. Harrington, C.J. Miller, J.F. O'Biern Thos. M. O'Donnell, F.C. Glidden, R.A. Boyle, W.T. O'Biern, J.H. Burke, M.J. Powers, C.L.P., E.A. Driscoll, H.J. Finn, M.J.C., Morris, Man, W.E. Lynch, A.E. Felton, J.A. Molloy, W.E. Hasty, T.J. O'Leary, E. Noonan, E.A. Coney, —Dalton, D.J. Donovan, W. Ford, — Shields, N.E. Cobb, J.A. Dougher, — Eldridge, — Kelly, P.F. Cronan, —Blanchard, H. McD., B.E. Brown, Cash, — Kelly, W.C. McCurdy, A.V. Loesan, — Gordon, Hazilboom, — Carroll, F.J. Flynn, J.J. Hart, H.C.W., W.C. Clinch, J.A. Driscoll, M.O. McAllen, Geo. M. Thomas, F.M. Smith, — Law, — Malone, W.A. Lewis, J.F. Burke, O.L. Barron, A.H. Nelson, G.J. McCram, J.F. Sheehan, C.H. Morse, H.L. Flynn, R.E. Tobin, E.T. Cohoon, C.C. White, C.A. Wardwell, — Terry, Geo J. McCarthy, Jas. Sullivan, K.A. Mahoney, J. Sullivan, M.A. Reardon, M.J. Nutter, J.P. O'Donohue, W. Costello,

The shells of gutted warehouses serve as a backdrop to the supplies of new lumber and building materials on the wharves, brought in to begin rebuilding the city.

Mr. Lang, Jas. Donovan, R. Harrington, Frank Smith, Peter Hughes, Peter Mooney, W.B. Desmond, Mr. P. Horn, J. Dearie, P. McCarthy, A Friend, R.L.S.P. Burke, Nellie Donovan, Arthur E. Carter.

The following-named persons contributed 20 cents each:

B. Callahan, R. King, P. Hooton. F.C.E., E.R. Piper, F. Wallace, J.H. Laudrey, F. Wallace.

The following-named persons contributed 10 cents each:

A Friend, E.A. Groves, L.B. Snow, W.F. Reed, Mr. Durret, W. Houllihan, Peter McFarlend, A Friend, M. Young, L. Stalel, P.M.L., Cash, E. Chemits, J. Brown, A.G.E.; A Friend.

Clothing Received.

There were many who contributed bundles of clothing, but omitted their names, either through delicacy or neglect.

Rev. Charles F. Sweet, 11 Camden Street, Lawrence; A Shuman & Co., E.H. Corey, Newton Highlands; Mrs. Vost, Milton, S.H. Root, 136 Summer St., Boston; Mrs. Dowe, Newton, Mass; W.G. Means, 248 Commonwealth Ave., Mr. and Mrs. P.J. Brazil; C.J. Simmons, Grove Hall; M.N. Fardy, 42 Hampden St.; Mr. E.R. Rand, Tyler St., Boston; Mr. T.R. Appleton, 8 Wyoming St., Boston; Miss Kate Tobin, H. Hastings, I.W.S. Winthrop, Emily Neal; E.J. Esterbrook, Newton; James H. Edgar, Brockton; Mrs. Ivers W. Adams; Mrs. S.A. Brown, Lake Crossing, Natick, Mass.; Miss Kate Rawlins, Hotel Lucerne, Boston; S. Lewis & Co., South Boston, a large kitchen range; Ladies' Domestic Missionary, Portsmouth, N.H.; Rev. Geo. P. Huntington, Hanover, N.H.; "Canadian"; Walter U. Lawson; Isable W. Sears Winthrop; Peabody, Mass.; Mr. J.N. Spalding, Brookline; Miss Clara Duchemin; Pilgrim Congregational Church, North Weymouth, per Rev. A.B. Hudson; King's Daughters, Cambridgeport; Miss Mary Ryan, Chester Square; Mrs. Lucy Stone; Mrs. Ellen Wyse, 65 Bedford St., New Bedford, Mass; M.W. Dooley; Samuel Chauncey, Stoneham; Mrs. Ford, A Friend; Mrs. Geo. Sutton; Mrs. Vickery; G. Pynn Mrs. D.F. Brien; Miss Lizzie Kiely; Mrs. Howard; Mrs. J.J. Dempsey; Edward T. Russell, from Portsmouth, N.H.; Mrs. A.O. Moore, Nicholas Ryan.

Miscellaneous Articles.

FROM BOSTON MERCHANTS.—Messrs. John Holman & Co., 25 mattresses; North Packing Company, 10 barrels beef; Messrs. C.A. Baldwin & Co., 4 barrels beef; Messrs. De Long, Seaman & Co., 8 ranges; from other parties, 4 bedsteads, 1 table, 12 chairs; Messrs. Swift Bros., 1 barrel pork; Messrs. Breed, Pierce & Co., 3 cases crystalline salt, 2 cases Wheat Germ meal; L.G. Burnham, Esq., 3 tons coal; Messrs. J.P. Harris & Co., Salem, 5 barrels flour; 1 barrel flour, from A friend.

Statement of the Fund For St. John's Fire Sufferers as Held By Edward T. Russell.

To cash received,	$8,036.33	
cr.		
Aug. 8 By paid John Holman & Co.:		
150 Husk Cot.top Matts., 4-4, No. 22, at $3.25,	$487.50	
10 Husk Cot.top Matts. 4-2, No. 22, at $3.25,	$32.50	
20 Husk Cot.top Matts., 3-0, No. 22, at $2.87 1/2,	57.50	
20 Husk. Cot-top Matts., 3-6, No. 22, at $3.00,	60.00	
45 6-yd. Mats, at 50c.,	22.50	$660.00
" paid Chas. A. Baldwin & Co.:		
25 Bbls. Plate Beef, at $7.00	$175.00	
20 Cases CC Beef, 12 1/2, at $1.65	33.00	
1 Bbl.,	.25	

19 Newcastle Hams, 346 — 19 = 327 lbs. at 12 1/2 c.,	40.88	249.13
"paid North Packing and Provision Co.:		
25 Bbls. Butt Pork, at $12.00,	300.00	
"paid Walker and Pratt Manuf. Co.:		
50 No. 7 Nelson Ranges, with pot, teakettle, spider, pot-covers, meat-pan, 1 sq. tin pan, at $13.00,	650.00	
"paid Smith and Anthony Stove Co.:		
60 Plain Hubs, 7 X 16, at $9.00,	$540.00	
60 Sets Furniture, at $1.75,	105.00	645.00
carried forward	$2,504.13	$8,036.33
Brought forward	$2,504.13	$8,036.33
Aug. 8. By paid Barstow Stove Co.:		
56 Ranges, 7 X 16, with hollowware, spiders, drip-pan, and bread-pan, at $13.00	728.00	
"paid Chas. W. Alley:		
131 Chairs, at $7.00	$76.41	
69 Chairs, at $9.00	51.75	
32 Rockers, at $11.00	29.33	
18 Rockers, at $13.50	20.25	
150 No. 934 Bedsteads, 4-4 ft., at $1.55,	232.50	
10 No. 934 Bedsteads, 4 ft. at $1.55	15.50	
20 No. 934 Bedsteads, 4 ft., at $1.55,	31.00	
20 No. 934 Bedsteads, 3 ft., at $1.55,	31.00	
		487.74
"paid Schooner *Carita*, Freight on above goods to Newfoundland	380.00	
Oct. 8 " paid Blaney, Brown, & Co.:		
625 Bbls Flour, at $4.00,	2,500.00	
25 Bbls. Beef, at $6.00	150.00	
37 Cases Beef, at $1.50	55.50	
"Freight and Insurance, Schooner *Alta*	462.70	
		$7,268.07
Expenses of Executive Committee,	390.43	
		$7,658.50
Balance in hands of Committee.		$377.83

Edward T. Russell
per W.P. Hewins.
Boston, Oct. 20, 1892.

The new Central Fire Station, shown here on its completion in 1895. This structure was built as a result of an inquiry by Judge D.W. Prowse. It is understood that prior to this a summer cottage—which was sometimes used by the Governor—was located on this site. Up to that time most, if not all, firemen were volunteers.

The following pages consist of advertisements, presumably used as a method of covering the cost of printing. We include them here as a matter of interest to the readers of today.

Copper Alloy

CHEAP TYPE

IS DEAR AT ANY PRICE

BUY THE BEST

THE MOST DURABLE TYPE IS

COPPER ALLOY

Type Metal

CAST AT THE

BOSTON * TYPE * FOUNDRY

104 MILK STREET,

BOSTON, MASS.

GOLD MEDAL, PARIS, 1878.

WALTER BAKER & CO.'S

Breakfast Cocoa,

FROM WHICH THE EXCESS OF OIL HAS BEEN REMOVED,

Is Absolutely Pure and it is Soluble.

No chemicals are used in its preparation. It has more than Three Times the Strength of cocoa mixed with Starch, Arrowroot or Sugar, and is therefore far more economical, Costing Less Than One Cent a Cup. It is delicious, nourishing, strengthening, Easily Digested, and admirably adapted for invalids as well as for persons in health.

ASK YOUR GROCER FOR IT. ALLOW NO SUBSTITUTION.

WALTER BAKER & CO.,

DORCHESTER, MASS,